Mia Marconi has an Italian father and an Irish mother. She grew up in London and has been a foster carer here for over 20 years. During that time she has welcomed more than 250 children into her home. To protect the identities of people she is writing under a pseudonym.

Also by Mia Marconi:

A Child Called Hope

The true story of a foster mother's love

Mia Marconi

HarperTrueLife

if Only He'd Told Me

A foster family pushed to the limits

Mia Marconi

HarperTrueLife

Little Girl Lost

The true story of a broken child

Mia Marconi

HarperTrueLife

Learning to Love Amy

Learning to Love Amy

The foster carer who saved a mother and a daughter

Mia Marconi

with Sally Beck

Certain details in this story, including names, places and dates, have been changed to protect the family's privacy.

HarperTrueLife
An imprint of HarperCollins*Publishers*
77–85 Fulham Palace Road,
Hammersmith, London W6 8JB

www.harpertrue.com
www.harpercollins.co.uk

First published by HarperTrueLife 2014

1 3 5 7 9 10 8 6 4 2

Mia Marconi and Sally Beck assert the moral right to be identified as the authors of this work

A catalogue record of this book is available from the British Library

PB ISBN: 978-0-00-810503-7
EB ISBN: 978-0-00-758441-3

Chapter One

It was a typical British day: rainy, black sky, lightning, with thunder claps so loud they made you jump. Janet and I didn't care; we were happy dancing away, singing at the tops of our voices while *Star Wars* played on a loop on the telly. Every so often Janet would sigh, 'I love Luke Skywalker, Mia. I really love him,' or she'd say, 'Mia. My Luke Skywalker, where is he?' And I would say, 'He's up there with the stars, looking for you.' Then we would collapse, laughing, and carry on dancing.

I wondered what a passerby looking through the front window would make of me whirling a Down's syndrome teenager round and round, both of us dancing inelegantly, giggling hysterically, while I tried to explain that Luke Skywalker only existed on the television screen. I was cheering her up, they would think, but the reverse was true. I know this sounds odd but Janet was a fantastic therapist to me, and came along just when I needed her.

I met Janet because she lived next door to us, with her lovely mum Lizzy and younger sister Emma. The first time I saw her I looked at her big, innocent smile and couldn't help but smile back. We hit it off straight away, which is unusual because Down's syndrome children are quite fussy and only interact with certain people, but I did not dismiss her as so many other people did, and Janet picked up on that. The look of relief on Lizzy's face when she realised her daughter was going to be accepted by us was a special moment.

'Thank you,' she mouthed silently at me.

'Janet is lovely,' I mouthed silently back.

Emma was six, the same age as my youngest daughter Ruby, and although my eldest, Francesca, was seven, and Janet fifteen, because of her disability Janet was oblivious to the fact that she was twice their age and joined in with all their games. I would often find them happily playing with Barbies, getting them ready to go to balls and parties.

Our family – Martin, Francesca, Ruby and I – had only recently moved into the house next to Janet and her family, and I believed that fate had led us there. I felt as though we had found exactly the right house at exactly the right time, because our old home was full of sadness after the sudden death of our foster child Hope. I had cried so many tears in that house, I felt the only real way to exorcise the sadness was to leave.

Learning to Love Amy

I know it's a funny thing to say about mere bricks and mortar, but the place we found was healing in a way I could never have predicted. Firstly, we had bought it from the local parish church, and the moment you walked through the door you were enveloped by a feeling of calm. It was like an invisible being wrapping their arms around you, whispering that everything was going to be okay. I felt safe, protected and secure for the first time in months. The irony was that after Hope's death I had craved the peace, tranquillity and silence of our local church, and now I got that same feeling in our new house.

It was in a quiet, tree-lined road with a large village-style green at the top. Priests had lived there and I was sure that was why its spiritual atmosphere was so strong. You could feel every prayer and every blessing that had ever been said there, as though all that love had been absorbed by the walls.

When I walked through the door that first time, I fell in love with it, totally oblivious to the amount of work that needed doing to make it habitable. The roof leaked and needed replacing; it would cost a fortune and had to be done fast, because when it rained out came the buckets. Me and the girls often slept in one room, giggling when we had to get up to empty them. Martin never saw the funny side – why would he? He had to do all the work – and slept next door where it was drier.

Martin looked at the bare walls and floorboards, and walked around muttering under his breath, 'What have we done? It needs new everything, and we don't have the money to do it!'

I just smiled and said, 'We will. We will be able to make this our home, and I promise you, it will be a happy one.'

I'd give him a big kiss, the girls would hug his legs, Jack and Jill (the dogs) would start licking his hand and he'd smile and walk off muttering again, pretending to be cross. As always, I was the optimist and Martin the pessimist. We were Yin and Yang, chalk and cheese, Tom and Jerry, and that's why we worked so well together.

We settled into a routine. Martin would spend all day driving his cab, then come home, have his dinner and start working on the house. I would take the girls to school, come home and start painting. After a few months we were making progress, the crumbling walls were replastered, the peeling paint was sanded down and our furniture was beginning to make it look homely.

We were in a lovely area in Kent and Lizzy and her family could not have been better neighbours.

Lizzy was slim, with light-brown hair and clear skin. She was cool, calm and collected, and never raised her voice – a quality I have never mastered, which I put down to my fiery Italian blood. Despite our differences, though, we had so much in common.

Her husband was Italian, like my dad, and she was an osteopath, so in a caring profession like me, and we both adored children.

We each had two kids and were devoted, caring mothers. The one difference between us when it came to parenting was that she did not believe in pushing her children. If Janet didn't feel like getting on the coach to go to college, Lizzy would say, 'Oh Janet, if you don't want to go you don't have to,' whereas I would have just shouted, 'Janet, get on the bus and put your seatbelt on!'

We all have our own parenting skills and ways of raising children, though, and Lizzy's kids were lovely, so whatever she was doing worked for her. That's one thing that never ceases to amaze me about families: how we can all do it so differently, but as long as your intentions are good and you lavish children with love and care, and respond when they need you, they seem to turn out fine.

Emma and Ruby became best friends and when the girls were home, Janet would dress up with them and they would all sit there playing with make-up and laughing. What was lovely to watch was how Emma, who was a shy little girl, began to accept Janet who, to be honest, she was a bit embarrassed to be seen with. At first, when Ruby and Francesca would say, 'Come on, Janet, come on, Emma; we're going up the shops,' Emma would tell Janet she couldn't come, but after a while, because Ruby and

Francesca treated Janet as though she had no disability, Janet began to tag along and Emma stopped being embarrassed by her Down's syndrome sister.

Janet and I had a wonderful connection and while the girls were at school, she was my best friend. Janet was a character. I loved her because she was brutally honest and had a simple approach to life and a straightforward way of talking. If she didn't like you she would tell you straight. She, in turn, loved that I treated her the same as I would anyone else. I have always had that ability; I don't care if you're the Queen or a tramp – everyone is equal in my eyes.

Some days, things that reminded me of Hope just seemed to haunt me. I'd find a toy that she had loved, and before I knew it I was in tears. When I felt really low thinking about Hope I would talk about her for hours to Janet, who would look me straight in the eye and say, 'Don't be stupid, Mia. Your stupid Hope is okay and you're with me now. Put the bloody kettle on.'

Then Janet would look at my puffy, tear-stained face and say, 'Mia, you look like crap. Hope is safe in heaven, you don't need to worry.'

I would laugh, immediately snap out of it, put the music on and we'd start dancing.

Normally, I love spending time outside the home, because I am a bit of a free spirit, but in the months after Hope died, I just wanted to stay in all the time, partly because I had so much to do in the house, what with all the painting, the waiting around for deliveries and catering for the workmen's never-ending tea breaks, and partly because I was still grieving and wanted to keep that private.

Grief is such a personal experience, one we all deal with in our own way. My way was to lock myself in my house with lovely, uncomplicated Janet, who possessed the ability not to judge me.

I felt judged by those close to me. Whether or not they really were being judgemental I don't know – no one ever said 'I told you so' or 'How irresponsi-ble' to my face – but I knew everyone thought Hope would be too much for me to cope with, and after she died, I felt they were all thinking, 'Well, what did she think the outcome was going to be?' because, deep down, that's how I felt. In quiet moments, when I was being honest with myself, I wondered exactly that. What had I been thinking when I agreed to care for such a sick little girl? If I had driven a car at a hundred miles an hour and crashed, people would have said, 'Well, what did you expect?' So how was this any different?

This time, being the eternal optimist who thinks they can fix everything didn't work. My character is to jump first and think afterwards. Mostly I come up smelling of roses, although with a few scratches, but this time was different. I had been well and truly ripped to shreds and I was spending a lot of time thinking about Hope.

Janet was new to my world, uncomplicated by prejudice, and I felt safe telling her how I felt because she wasn't going to judge me or give me advice. She did the most important thing and that was to listen.

'Sorry for crying,' I remember saying so often to her.

'That's okay, Mia,' she would say before changing the subject.

For Janet, this was the first time anyone had really needed her. We all like to be needed and Janet was no exception, but because of her disability people felt uncomfortable confiding in her. Now she felt she had a friendship on an equal footing, and she dealt with it on her terms, not mine.

The house was honestly a mess, with its peeling wallpaper, years and years of paintwork that needed sanding and that interminably dripping roof. Martin and I were both working so hard we were truly exhausted, and one afternoon the tiredness just seemed to creep into every bone in my body. There was nothing for it; I just lay down on my bed for a nap. Next thing I knew, Lizzy was banging on my door, shouting, 'Mia, Mia. Are you there?'

Waking up with a start, I realised I'd missed the school run. It was so unlike me – normally I was one of the first mums in the playground.

'Are the girls all right?' I said as I raced out the door.

Learning to Love Amy

'They're fine, they're in the Head's office,' I could just hear Lizzy say as I raced to the school at what felt like a hundred miles an hour.

I got to the Head's office and looked at their long faces, which were as dejected as a pair of lost puppies'. I felt terrible and made up for it by cuddling them all the way home and buying them a huge ice cream.

This was so out of character for me; not just forgetting to pick up Francesca and Ruby, but falling asleep in the middle of the day. I did have umpteen jobs, I reasoned, and had just moved and was still grieving, so maybe that was it. Then, suddenly, the realisation that I could be pregnant slapped me hard in the face. I said nothing, though, and kept it to myself for the time being.

It was perfectly possible, as I wasn't using any contraception. Martin and I worked out the times in the month when I was likely to get pregnant and didn't have sex then, and that method had worked well so far. But we were so busy that keeping track of the day was hard enough, never mind when I was ovulating. Secretly, I wanted more children, and I had never really let on to Martin how big I wanted my family to be. One thing I knew was that I just loved being a mum, because there is no feeling quite like it, and no one can prepare you for how much you are going to love your children. When I was flying around the world with my job it would never have occurred to me to give it up, but now I was a mum it never occurred to me to go back. Whatever would be, as far as family was concerned, would be. I embraced and enjoyed every minute.

The following morning, Lizzy dropped Janet off with me before the college coach arrived as she had a hospital appointment, and anyway Janet did not want to go to college because she was feeling ill. She was well enough to come on the school run with me, and after we dropped the girls off I walked round to the chemist to get a pregnancy test.

Back home, I ran straight into the bathroom, did the test and held my breath. Those two positive blue lines appeared immediately. I was so excited and so was Janet, and we danced around the living room, singing, 'I'm going to have a baby, I'm going to have a baby.'

Janet celebrated by pushing a cushion up her jumper and asking, 'If it's a boy, can you call him Luke Skywalker?'

It was winter at the time and freezing cold outside, so I made a flask of soup, buttered a roll, wrapped the pregnancy test in foil and put it inside the roll, with the ends sticking out so you could just about see it, then I drove to the cab stand where I knew Martin would be taking his break. He looked cold and tired, so the soup was a godsend. He also looked confused.

'Everything all right?' he said.

'Yes, fine. Just thought you might need something warming,' I said, trying hard not to smile and give myself away.

I hadn't had much time for him recently, so he wondered what on earth I was doing there. I didn't wait; I kissed him on the cheek and left.

Until I did the test, I'd had absolutely no clue that I was pregnant. In fact, I couldn't even remember having sex! However hard I racked my brain, I just could not remember. One thing was for sure, it was not the Immaculate Conception, and I made a note to take contraception more seriously.

When Martin came through the door that night he had the biggest smile on his face. He walked straight over and gave me a huge hug. Later that evening we told the girls, who were absolutely delighted, and in that moment I knew that whatever road we travelled together, we would be all right. Life could not have been better, I thought, but then I had thought that before.

Once the excitement had died down, all I could think was how on earth we were going to get the house ready in time. My second thought was that I hoped it was a girl, although I knew Martin was desperate for a boy.

We were in a good place, though, and the time was right. The girls loved the new house and they were doing brilliantly at school, which reported that they were happy and blossoming, and that all trace of the sadness they had suffered after Hope had died was gone. The neighbours loved them and they were the new kids on the block.

I called my mum. 'Are you sitting down?'

'What's happened?' Mum said, a slight panic in her voice.

'It's all good, don't worry. We're having a baby!'

'It's so funny you should say that – I was just wondering if you and Martin were planning to have more. I can't wait to be a nan again!'

My whole family were overjoyed, but particularly Mum, because she had suffered a horrific shock a few weeks earlier. She had always been a tower of strength to me, and had seen me crumble after Hope's death, but recently it had been her turn to be heartbroken.

Mum's older sister Lily had had an only son called Joseph, who was more like a brother to Mum than a nephew, as they were so similar in age. No one knew why, but he had committed suicide. One morning he got up early, attached a hosepipe to the exhaust of his car and fed it through the window, knowing perfectly well that the carbon monoxide fumes would kill him. That day, the bottom fell out of Mum and Auntie Lily's world.

After Joseph's funeral, Lily's whole appearance was transformed, partly because of grief, and partly

because of the medication she was taking to anaes-
thetise herself from the grief.

It was about six months after Joseph's suicide
when Mum called and I could barely understand
what she was saying, she was sobbing so hard.

'What's happened, Mum? Take a deep breath and
tell me what it is.'

It took a minute for Mum to compose herself.
'Lily's dead,' she managed to blurt out between sobs.

I was speechless. All I could say for the next
minute or so was, 'Mum, I am so, so sorry. Stay
where you are. I'm coming round.'

I don't think any of us were that surprised to hear
about Auntie Lily. It wasn't suicide exactly, but the
post-mortem showed that a mix of tranquillisers and
white wine killed her. To numb the pain, Lily was
drinking two bottles a day and had probably forgotten how many pills she had taken – a combination
that proved lethal.

Facing two funerals in quick succession was painful
for everyone, and only a year after Hope's death.
Deep down I knew the sadness couldn't last and that
something would come along to lift the family's spirits, and it was my pregnancy. The timing of it could
not have been more perfect.

It was brilliant news as far as my family were
concerned and everyone got really excited. The
phone never stopped. Everybody got involved,

suggesting names, wondering if it was a boy or a girl (everyone hoped for a boy because that's what Martin wanted) or saying, 'Is there anything you need? What can we get you?' It wasn't just between Martin and me; it was a family event, and everyone embraced it. Finally, we had something to smile about and something other than the death of Lily and Joseph to talk about.

As I ticked off the months my bump grew bigger and bigger, and the new house took shape. Family and friends helped us decorate, but the most special helper was my beloved dad.

Dad did everything for me and I could do no wrong in his eyes. If I'd come home and said, 'Dad, I've just murdered someone,' he'd have said, 'Go and get me the shovel.' His love was unconditional, and we just needed to look at each other to know what the other was thinking. I was never going to feel as special with anyone as I did with my dad, I knew that, so I treasured these moments.

I had an extremely supportive family willing to do anything for me without expecting anything in return, and that fact did not escape me. Dad wanted nothing for the hours and hours of work he put in. The only thing he would accept was a glass of chilled white Italian wine at the end of the day and fish and chips on a Friday night.

They were fun times and special times. We would laugh, and shout at each other if we messed up. I loved it when it was just me, Dad, the bump and the paint roller.

Nine months flew by and my waters broke one Saturday while I was up a ladder, painting the hall-way. Dad and Martin were both there, Dad painting the other side of the hall, with Martin working on the top floor.

Dad shouted up to him: 'Mia's labour's started!'

Martin panicked, slipped downstairs and landed in a heap at the bottom. While he lay there groaning, Dad was running round like a headless chicken and I was crippled with contractions. It was like a sketch from a sitcom, only no one was laughing.

Somehow we composed ourselves and Dad prom-ised to look after Francesca and Ruby while Martin drove me to the hospital.

The car journey was horrendous – Martin was useless, and we rowed all the way. He was driving about twenty miles an hour and it didn't help that Saturday shoppers were out in force, and when he stopped at a red light I finally lost it.

'For heaven's sake, go through it and drive faster!' I shouted.

'I don't want to get a ticket!' Martin replied.

'Are you off your head? I'm having a baby!'

We finally arrived and I was so far into my labour I had lost the ability to walk.

'Run and get a wheelchair,' I managed to puff between contractions.

When Martin got back I was screaming, but somehow he managed to get me into the chair. Finally, he shot off like a Formula 1 racing driver, speeding through three sets of double doors, all of them closed, so by the time we reached the labour ward not only was I crippled with contractions, but my shins were black and blue, too.

'*Now* you decide to put your foot down!' I said, and he ignored me.

Isabella was born fifteen minutes later.

Martin was so fed up that he didn't have a son, he reached into my overnight bag and chucked the pink Babygro and blanket I'd put in there out of the window, and a nurse had to run down and rescue them.

I had a bit of sympathy for him because being surrounded by us girls, with no interest in football or car mechanics, must have been hard for him at times. I knew how I would long for a girl if I only had sons, so when I saw the blanket go flying, I smiled to myself.

The lovely thing about Martin is that he never stays mad for long. It's true for both of us, really; we'll have a row, shout and scream, and then it's all out in the open and forgotten about a few minutes later.

'I'm getting a cuppa,' he said, still looking sulky, and ten minutes later he returned with the biggest bunch of flowers I have ever seen and a packet of Jaffa Cakes, my favourite biscuit.

I was cuddling Isabella.

'Can I hold her?' he asked.

'Idiot,' I said. 'Course you can.'

He scooped her up gently, and although he tried to hide it, I could see tears welling up in his eyes. As he stood cooing at her, holding her tiny hand, I promised I would buy Isabella a Chelsea football club Babygro, got off the bed and limped over to give him a hug.

'You still in pain?' the nurse asked.

'Only my shins,' I said, and she looked confused.

I left hospital after a few hours and by the time I got home the family were there waiting, so I could forget any thoughts of having a rest. The chatter and laughter was so loud I'm sure the whole neighbourhood heard, and the house looked like a florist's shop.

Chapter Two

A few days later the doorbell went and I was surprised to see Peter, my social worker, on the doorstep with another huge bunch of flowers.

'Congratulations,' he smiled.

The last time he had seen our family we were on the floor with grief, so it was good for him to see us looking happy. Hope's death had an impact on him, too, and I know he felt guilty about what our family had gone through. After all, it was he who suggested Hope came to live with us.

We chatted for a while, but not about fostering, although I'm sure he wanted to. I still had no thoughts of fostering again, and there was no hint then that anything was about to change.

Soon after moving into the new house, I had met another foster carer who lived locally, a lovely lady called Martine. Martine had begun caring because she was unable to have children of her own, and although she and her husband had gone through the adoption process, they had been unable to adopt a child. They wanted a baby – something all childless couples prefer – but the reality is that babies rarely come up for adoption. In fact, it's rare to be able to adopt a child under two. Then they had split up, so Martine decided fostering was the next best thing.

I assumed she and her husband had divorced because they couldn't have kids, but one day Martine told me the shocking true story.

'You might find this out from other people, so I might as well tell you myself,' Martine said. 'After the adoption failed, my husband started seeing another woman and then got her pregnant. That's why we divorced.'

'Martine, I am so, so sorry,' I said, thinking how I could never imagine Martin doing anything like that, even if we had not been able to have children.

Martine was fostering a little girl called India, who was an accommodated child, which basically means that her mother had voluntarily put her into care. She was her first foster daughter and Martine confided in me that she had been overjoyed at the prospect of helping India recover from a terrible start in life.

'I wanted to make it right for her. I thought we would have fun days out at the park, lots of love and cuddles on the sofa, sipping hot chocolate and watching *Dumbo*,' she said. 'But Mia, I don't know if it's me or if it's India, but she seems scared of me.'

'Why? You are the kindest person on the planet. I don't understand.'

'I don't either and I don't know what to do.'

I had noticed a distance between India and Martine but thought that was just because she was settling in.

Martine began to tell me India's story and little by little I began to understand. India was almost three years old and her mother, Amy, had put her through hell. Amy was a chaotic alcoholic who lived in squalor and was incapable of looking after herself, let alone parenting her daughter. Mother and daughter were known to social services, who had done their best to help Amy sort out her life. They had started by sending a specialist company to cleanse Amy's disgusting flat. I saw photos of it later and there were piles of dirty clothes covering every surface, half-eaten plates of food and rubbish bags spilling their contents across the carpet. The mess was appalling and almost obscured the empty vodka bottles that littered the place. It was a shock to see them everywhere, and an even bigger shock that they weren't the first things you noticed.

One thing not in the photos was the drunks who spent their days there, drinking with Amy until they were unconscious. Amy's place wasn't so much a crack den, but an alcoholics' den, and because she was a mum she had her own place, whereas most of the others were sleeping rough. It was no wonder they all loved hanging out at Amy's, and she was grateful for the company.

If Amy went out to the park it was not to the swings; she joined other drinkers on park benches, and they sat nursing cans of strong lager or cider while India watched, strapped into her pushchair. 'A dog couldn't live in those conditions,' I thought to myself, 'never mind a child.'

Amy had chosen vodka and a can of Special Brew over her own child. What mother would do that? But alcohol had a strong hold over her and no one could compete.

Despite more than enough support and lessons in domestic management, Amy never mastered keeping the place clean. Social services couldn't perpetually send in cleaners, and they were receiving a lot of concerned phone calls about India, from one family member in particular.

If Amy couldn't clean up her act, sooner or later social services would have to act to protect India. In fact, even while Amy was attempting to be a domestic goddess, they suspected she would fail and were actively seeking an interim care order.

To pre-empt the humiliation of having India taken away, which would mean the police turning up at her door with a social worker and a court order and forcing Amy to hand her over, in a sober moment Amy decided India would be better off in care. It was the right thing to do and must have been hard, so to give Amy her due, she did put India first for once.

India showed no signs of physical abuse, but she must have been hurting inside. There was no Cinderella law to protect her from emotional neglect and free her from the daily routine of caring for her mother; she just had to get on with it or she would get shouted at.

India's days with Amy would have gone something like this:

'India, Mummy's tired, get me a blanket.'

'India, Mummy's got a headache, don't make any noise.'

'India, Mummy's hungry, get me something to eat.'

'India, I don't want to watch this film, find something that Mummy likes.'

It would have started as soon as India was able to toddle and understand simple commands. Amy was merely copying the way she had been raised and knew no different.

Consequently, Amy was needy, and India learned from a very early age that simple things like food, toys, bath times or even bed times were not considered important. Her needs were never met, she realised, so she simply stopped asking and tried to disappear into the background.

So it was no surprise that she arrived at Martine's with more emotional baggage than a camel could carry.

To look at India, the only thing that gave away that she wasn't like other little girls was her solemn face. Other than that she had bright blue eyes, long dark hair and a vulnerable air that made you want to protect her. Martine was no different and gave her a big cuddle the minute they were introduced, but instead of returning it, India froze and went as stiff as a board. It was awkward. Martine was not prepared to be rejected and felt humiliated and embarrassed.

'She obviously doesn't like me, Mia, and I don't know what to do.'

I didn't know what to say. 'Just give it time, Martine. She probably just needs time to settle in.'

'You're probably right,' Martine said, but she didn't look convinced.

If Martine was finding dealing with India hard, she found dealing with Amy impossible. Martine was from a hard-working family who just happily got on with their lives, not bothering anyone else. Amy was volatile, difficult and destructive, and Martine had no clue how to manage her. As India was placed in care voluntarily and Amy was at liberty to see her daughter whenever she liked, Martine had to deal with her all the time, and Amy had clearly decided she was not going to make it easy.

There were rules, but Amy always thought they didn't apply to her, and even if she hadn't thought that, she would have broken them anyway. She was supposed to arrange with Martine and social services

23

when she could see India, but she never did, instead turning up drunk at Martine's house whenever she felt like it. An undignified tussle always followed, with Amy screaming at Martine and Martine trying her best to calm her down. Poor India looked on bewildered, and as much as Martine tried to protect her, she knew exactly what was going on. You can imagine how India's loyalties were torn in two; her instinct would have told her to support her mum, however awful she was. She would have felt like she was betraying her mum if she formed a close relationship with someone Amy obviously didn't like. Even aged three, India knew that blood is thicker than water.

Things got out of hand one day when Amy accused Martine of trying to take her child away. It obviously wasn't true and Martine tried hard to explain that she was simply taking care of India until Amy felt better, but Amy wasn't listening.

I'd seen it all before, but Martine had never been exposed to such behaviour before. Whenever I saw her at the toddler group we both went to, she looked exhausted and fragile, and I noticed the awkwardness between her and India. They were very formal together, more like pupil and teacher than carer and child.

'Would you like a juice, India?' Martine would say.

'No,' India would reply, avoiding Martine's eyes.

If she was struggling on the climbing frame and Martine went to help her, India would simply get down and run away. Martine was right: clearly India had not taken to Martine, and Martine, try as she might, could not connect with India.

Being placed with a single mum with no other children – the mirror image of the situation she had left – did not help this neglected little girl feel comfortable. Her mother was unpredictable and she had no concept that not all single women were like Mummy.

Fostering was a world away from what Martine expected. She was looking for emotional fulfilment and she wasn't getting that – quite the opposite, in fact – so all in all she felt a failure, and after five months she was ready to give in.

One day she again confided in me.

'I don't think I can do this any more, Mia. I am getting absolutely nowhere. I am going to have to tell social services I can't go on.'

I agreed with her. 'Honestly, I think you have done everything you can.'

'Do you really?' she said, her eyes filling with tears. 'I just don't think fostering is for me.'

'It's not for everyone,' I said, giving her a hug. 'Don't be too hard on yourself.'

The high-octane, unpredictable life of foster caring was not right for Martine, so she told social services she would care for India until they found her a new home. India was to be Martine's first and last placement.

Martine's fallout with Amy and her subsequent decision to give up fostering coincided with an earth-shattering international event. It was 1990, and Romania was in the news because of a child scandal that shocked the world. The Ceauşescu regime had outlawed birth control, with the result that families were giving birth to children they could not afford to keep. Parents already struggling financially felt they had no choice but to abandon their unwanted sons and daughters and in desperation took them to be cared for in state orphanages. The only problem was that the State had no money to care for them either, so that often as many as 700 children could be crammed into a filthy hovel masquerading as a children's home. It was inhumane, and horrific news footage broadcast distressing scenes of unimaginable neglect. One film showed four babies, looking haunted and unloved, sharing a rusty metal cot. The only stimulation they had was to bang their heads on the bars. Another showed toddlers tied to their beds, rocking back and forth, with no one there to help them. They had little food, were rarely changed and no one to talk to them or love them. I was so upset I cried my eyes out for weeks.

We were all outraged and shocked, and Martine was no different. She felt she had to act and made up her mind to go to Romania to adopt two children. I supported her in whatever way I could, and part of that support was taking over the care of India.

I already knew India, and because I had passed the relevant checks from the Criminal Records Bureau I was already Martine's support worker, allowed to look after India when Martine needed a stand-in. Gradually, it began to make sense that I should take over India's care.

Before I did, though, I spoke to Martin and the girls about whether we should foster again and whether we were ready to open our arms to help those who needed us. They thought we were, because although what had happened with Hope was terrible, there had been about twenty other children between Yasmin, my first foster child, and her, and those placements had all been fine. And I kept thinking that if Hope were here, she would want me to carry on.

I spoke to Peter. I loved Peter, because he was very supportive, understanding and gentle – the perfect social worker, really. He had a good relationship with the girls and got on well with Martin, and we spoke at great length about our strengths as a family.

We concluded that although we weren't perfect, we were stable, loving and we communicated well. Martin and I would row, but all the kids – ours and the foster children – knew that we were just clearing the air; we were not going to separate and arguing didn't have to equal violence. If things got to boiling point in the house – which is inevitable in any family, big or small – I would shout, 'Family time!' and we would all sit round the kitchen table, taking turns to air our grievances. The rules in our house were very clear. It was fine not to agree with everyone and to have different likes, dislikes and opinions; what was not fine was any kind of destructive or violent behaviour. No one was allowed to kick, punch, spit or smash up their room, and anyone crossing those lines faced consequences.

'Listen, I know it's something that means a lot to you, and, if I'm honest, I quite like having a houseful of kids, even if they're not mine,' Martin said, supporting me like he always does.

My mum was against it and worried about me continually, but that's mums. Deep down she knew I had a strong calling and was not going to stand in my way, so in the end she said, 'You know I will help out where I can. I'm proud of you for wanting to help these poor kids. God knows, they need someone.'

I had thought about giving up foster caring, but there was nothing else I wanted to do. There is something so rewarding, fulfilling and uplifting about it, and I was not ready to stop. There didn't seem any point in giving it up either, especially now I knew that India needed a new home.

India already knew me, and she loved the girls and the dogs, so it was natural that she would end up living with us. Also Isabella, who was seven months old by now, was such a good baby she was hardly any work at all, and when Ruby and Francesca were home I never got a look-in anyway.

Once we had all agreed, I got a little buzz of anticipation. I was ready to love another child again. India needed all the love she could get and I told myself that our family would do our best to help her get over the trauma she had suffered. We would treat her like one of the family and do everything we could to help her.

Social services thought it was a good idea, too, so it was time to tell India. Martine and I were in the park with Ruby, Francesca, Jack and Jill when we broke the news and her little round face lit up. Martine looked crushed momentarily, then looked at me with sad eyes and smiled.

'I like your dogs, Mia,' India said quietly.

'And they like you too, darling. Would you like to take them for a walk on a lead one day?'

India nodded her head vigorously and then skipped off to play on the swings with Ruby and Francesca.

It was a planned move, which I knew was rare in the world of emergency placements, and we began having conversations with India about Martine having to go to Romania to rescue some babies.

Chapter Three

The whole prospect of moving really thrilled India, and it was lovely to see her showing some emotion. She knew our home and she knew me, but her excitement wasn't because she was coming to live with me – I was realistic about that; it was because she loved playing with the girls. She felt safe around children; you could tell that immediately.

The week before India was due to come and live with us was really exciting. The girls helped me get her room ready: Ruby picked out a Barbie doll she thought India would like, and Francesca picked out a jigsaw puzzle with dogs on it and helped me put India's My Little Pony duvet cover on her bed.

The minute the bed was made, Jack and Jill jumped onto it.

'Naughty dogs!' giggled Ruby, before picking Jill up and cuddling her. Then the questions started.

'Does India like *Winnie-the-Pooh* videos?'

'Does she like making cakes? Can we make one with her tomorrow? Please, Mummy, please!'

After school the following day, Martine knocked at the door and Ruby and Francesca ran to answer it.

'Hello, India,' they chorused, as India hid nervously behind Martine.

'Come in, India,' I said.

She arrived with one small suitcase, which also had My Little Pony on it, and I thought to myself, 'That's all her worldly possessions.' I thought about Ruby and Francesca's bulging toy box, full of things their grandparents, aunts and uncles had bought them, and felt sad that not all children knew what it was like to be at the heart of a loving family.

India ran upstairs with Ruby and Francesca to look at her bedroom, which was full of pink frills, cuddly toys and a bookshelf full of books, and I could hear their excited chatter as I made Martine a cup of tea.

When she came down I said, 'Did you like it?'

'Yes, Mia,' she said shyly.

Martine and I exchanged glances, chatted for an hour over a cup of tea, then she said, 'Time for me to go, India.'

If India was going to cry at all it would have been then, but her eyes were dry and all she said was, 'Bye, Martine.'

'Bye, India.'

And that was it. She turned and left. What else could she do?

India came back inside and sat down quietly on the sofa.

There was no need to give her a list of rules; she was coming from another carer, not directly from a chaotic home, and Martine would have highlighted to me if she punched, kicked or swore – all reasons to lay down the law. And she would learn how we did things in our house from Ruby and Francesca, like shutting the toilet door and taking your wellies off before coming into the house.

The girls would be her safety net, her soft bean-bag, to lean on when she needed to. She would rarely have to be on her own with me – I understood from Peter and Martine that this could be uncomfortable for her – so I chatted to her from a distance and didn't move into her space unless she wanted me to. India felt safe at our house, I could tell, but I wondered if I would ever see her really relax and let go.

I would have to do some unravelling, because India never spoke about Amy, or Martine for that matter – she had blocked them from her mind, so I had little to go on.

I wait for children to talk about things when they feel comfortable, and they do that when you least expect it. The important thing is to leave colouring pens and spare paper out, where they can easily access it if they need to. Often they find it easier to draw what is bothering them than to talk about it. Talking about feelings is a skill you develop over time, but most children don't have it. If a child has something to say about a trauma it usually starts with something like, 'Mummy gets cross if I don't wash up properly.' It's a simple statement, which you need to investigate gently with questions like, 'Does Mummy shout when she gets cross or does she smack?' That's when you can find out whether parents are really abusive or not. There was no simple statement from India, for now, Amy was firmly packed away in a box. India made no move towards the pens and paper and she didn't talk about what happened at home either.

First, I concentrated on the basics. Amy had never provided India with any structure or routine, so for Martine, and now me, the first job was to try to turn that around.

Martine had worked hard to introduce her to routines and it was up to me to continue what she had started, but unlearning set behaviours is much harder than learning them.

Martine had managed to get India to sit at the table, but at dinnertime she was quieter than a sleeping baby, as eating at the table with a family was a new experience for her. She was so different to my family, who chatted noisily about their school day, laughing and occasionally crying. She'd had no mealtime routine with Amy at all; Amy had no dinner table or chairs, no clean plates, cutlery or glasses, so how could she have? India had no experience of family chat, no one to squabble with over the last roast potato, there had been no laughter and no tears. Dinner for India would have meant sitting in a corner with a packet of crisps or a slice of bread, and some days she might not even have had that. If it hadn't been for her family network, she could have starved to death.

At dinnertime in our house there was no corner India could hide in and it was a frightening time for her. Little by little she got used to it, but it was months before her confidence grew sufficiently so that she would actually speak.

Then came bedtime. After I'd put Isabella down, it was time for India's bath. I filled it full of Barbie dolls so I never had a problem getting her in. She might have found getting undressed awkward, but the girls were nearby so she could hear them laughing, singing and getting ready to go to sleep, and that reassured her.

A clean bed was something India had never experienced until she lived with Martine and she absolutely loved it. At Amy's she slept on a bare mattress with no sheet and a duvet with no cover, and pillows were alien – she never saw one until she moved into foster care.

Once in bed, I would sit next to her on a chair (mindful that she hated anyone getting too close) and read her a story, and she would listen intently, her bright blue eyes getting wider and wider every time I turned a page. I loved bedtimes, as it was one-to-one time that India didn't find threatening.

India absolutely loved books, almost more than any child I have ever seen. Her favourite stories were *The Velveteen Rabbit*, the classic story about the rabbit who wants the love of his owner to bring him to life, and the *Brambly Hedge* books about families of little mice – happy books, where she could escape from memories of her chaotic and sad world.

She trusted books. They never let her down. She could cuddle them in bed, but they showed no emotion back so were safe for India. Once her eyes closed, I would creep out, leaving the night light on, as she hated being in the dark. Then I would go and read to Ruby and Francesca. The experience was so different as they would cuddle up to me, asking questions about the story and laughing at the funny bits.

India was a pretty, chubby little girl who always looked anxious and apprehensive, but it was her mop of waist-length hair that you noticed first.

Head lice loved India's hair and resolutely set up camp there. I remember Martine explaining to me in grisly detail how it took her months and months to get rid of the lice when she'd first arrived. She said she could literally see them jumping out of her hair, and the social worker said it was the worst case of nits she had ever seen.

It was no surprise that India had a problem with her hair being brushed. Anything to do with her hair was traumatic, in fact; she hated hairbands, clips, bows, but especially hairbrushes. Growing up with Amy she would not have been bathed or washed very often, and even if she tried to wash herself, at age three she was too little to tackle her hair.

She still had nits when she came to me, and going near her with a hairbrush was a major exercise. It didn't matter whether I got princess brushes, pink brushes or soft brushes; India did not want one near her head. Consequently, washing her hair was a nightmare. She screamed from start to finish and afterwards it took about thirty minutes to brush the knots out, and by the end of it we were all exhausted. The irony was that hair-wash night was the *only* time India would get emotional as most of the time she was very quiet, so it was doubly distressing to see her get so upset.

Eventually, we solved the problem with a trip to the hairdresser, who cut India's hair into a lovely, manageable bob. This may sound obvious, and Martine had tried to do just that, but as India had been placed in care voluntarily, Amy had to give her permission for India to get a haircut, and she'd absolutely refused. Eventually, after weeks of asking, I got her to see sense and she agreed.

Playtime is so important to children for all sorts of reasons. It's sociable, teaches them various skills and, above all, makes them happy. It's lovely to watch little girls absorbed playing with a dolls' house or a cooking set and to hear their chatter as they decide what to make for dinner or which doll is sleeping where. They act everything out through play and I was keen for India to start, especially as she had spent so little time with other children.

Francesca and Ruby were excited to include her in their games, but at first, India watched them from a distance, occasionally smiling and giggling to herself with her face hidden behind a book. The girls didn't push her to play; they simply showed her how to do it. Little by little, India made small steps, joining in their dressing-up games and playing babies and animal hospitals with all their cuddly toys, or they would read together, discussing and laughing at the story. The girls had had to coax her at first, but before long she was enjoying her first real experience of being a child.

India eventually took up their offer to dress up as ET, or an imaginary model. Make-up was always involved and practically every night I found India looking like ET in drag.

Having make-up put all over her was a huge step forward because she was being touched and enjoying it. Getting it off was slightly trickier – I made sure I did it as gently as I could with cotton wool and make-up remover.

India was an easy child in a lot of ways because she demanded so little attention. Once she was happy playing with Francesca and Ruby, my job was relatively painless. But because she showed so little emotion – a mechanism she had learned to survive – she was also a closed book, which made it tough to read what she was thinking and feeling. She was also fearful of doing anything wrong, so scared of making a mistake that she wouldn't even try. No doubt Amy had screamed and shouted if India hadn't done what she asked, and I had to teach her that it was okay to make mistakes and okay to try, even if you had no idea of the outcome.

When she was about five, it was so hot we planned a day at the beach. It was a typical family day, with Francesca and Ruby singing and arguing in the car, and Martin getting more and more frustrated. We got there just in time and the girls jumped onto the beach, pulling off their dresses and rushing down to the sea in their mermaid bikinis. India refused to move, clinging to the steps as if her life depended on it.

'Come on, darling, take off your sandals.'

'I'm not!' she screamed.

'Come on, I'll carry you.' But each time I tried to put her down it was like I was putting her feet on hot coals.

It was getting embarrassing now and people were beginning to stare.

I carried India into the sea and she began screaming that the water was burning her. I couldn't work out what she meant but carried her back, dried her off and took her for a long walk.

We walked for miles but she wouldn't hold my hand, as she could tell I was getting annoyed. We sat on the grass.

'You okay, India?'

'Yes,' she replied, but her sullen face suggested otherwise.

The penny finally dropped. She had never experienced sand beneath her feet or sea water on her body. It was a new experience – the crowds, the heat, the idea of a family day out.

'Let's get an ice cream,' I said, and stuck a huge 99 Flake in it and covered it with strawberry sauce.

India looked lost.

'Next time, we can build a sand castle,' I said, and realised that on this occasion I hadn't got it right.

However inexperienced she was, she did want to join in with family life. India loved the dogs, and followed me round, watching me with her large, soft, inquisitive eyes, and if I was hanging out the washing or doing the hoovering she would imitate me. I made sure she had her own mini-hoover that was exactly the same as mine, and we set up a washing line in her bedroom that she could hang her dolls' clothes on.

India was eager to learn and eager to please, which sounds ideal, but people-pleasing was a habit she had acquired in order to survive. The easy option was to let her stay quiet and compliant, but I knew I had to get her to show the person she really was.

Sometimes I caught her unawares, and the first time she had a birthday cake was one. When she saw her cake come through the door covered with pink icing and candles, her blue eyes began to sparkle and she could not help smiling, but she found it daunting, too, and pretty soon burst into tears.

Kids being kids, the girls took over, blew India's candles out and opened her presents as she sat at a distance, watching. Anyone looking on would have thought it was their birthday, but she learned from them how to act and eventually got the hang of celebrations.

Chapter Four

When Martine said she was going to Romania, I was genuinely happy to support her in any way that I could, and taking India had been part of that. Secretly, I wanted to board the plane with her and rescue as many of those poor orphaned children as I could. It was such a big story and every week in the news lorries left the UK headed for Eastern Europe, loaded with food, toys and blankets to take to far-flung corners of Romania. It wasn't just the usual charities sending aid, either; the whole country got involved. The only silver lining when it came to Romania was watching the human spirit unfold as we all reacted and rose to the challenge.

Martine was so brave. The humiliation inflicted on her by her ex-husband needed courage and determination to repair, and she was convinced that this was the way to do it.

Months went by without any news. People asked around but no one had heard anything of Martine. Then one day, out of the blue, walking down my path with a double buggy, was a beautiful woman with her head held high. It was Martine, almost unrecognisable, as she looked so happy, pushing two tiny bundles, one wrapped up in a pink blanket and the other in a blue. She was back from Romania and had adopted twins: a boy and a girl, just six weeks old. She introduced me with a smile that said, 'I'm so happy I could burst.'

I hugged her so tightly I thought I might crush her.

'These are my babies,' she said.

'They are so gorgeous, and do you know something? I think they look like you.' Laughing, I opened the door and pushed the double buggy inside, ecstatic that her dream had come true. India was excited, too, although you might have thought she would react badly.

Children are more clued-up than we imagine, and India had worked out and accepted that she was not the child for Martine. So when she met Martine's two Romanian orphans her only reaction was joyful.

Poor India had no biological dad around. In fact, she had no idea who he was; Amy claimed not to know, which was perfectly possible because she was in such a state of drunkenness most of the time she did not always remember who she had slept with. Pregnancy had made no difference to the way Amy lived her life. You would have thought she might swap vodka for herbal tea, just for nine months, as she knew drinking alcohol could harm her baby, but she didn't. She didn't give up smoking, either. She would wake up in the mornings, and instead of a cup of tea, she would have vodka and orange and a cigarette. To Amy, orange juice in her vodka represented her five-a-day.

I was amazed that India had been born unscathed; she could have suffered all sorts of defects. I've always said that drinking while you're pregnant is like playing Russian roulette; you never quite know if you will get away with it.

Although India had been born physically healthy, her emotional development was topsy turvy. Amy had always treated her the same as an adult and I knew I would have to teach India how to be a child. Childhood is the one time in your life when you should have no worries, but India had never known that. So over those first few months, the first thing India had learned was to play without fear. When Amy was hungover, which was most days, if India had a noisy toy it could be whisked off her at any moment. And in any case, social services only found two things in Amy's flat suitable for a child to play with – a grubby Bob the Builder doll and a single saucepan – so toys had no good associations for India.

Bedtime had also been very difficult for her at first – more than for most children – and she needed to learn to sleep without getting angry.

'Time for bed,' I'd say in a sing-song voice, so that it sounded like fun.

'No, Mia, I'm not going,' India would say.

'We all have to sleep, India. If we don't we get grumpy and can't enjoy the day.'

'Well, I hate sleeping,' she would say before bursting into tears.

It was an anxious time for India because with Amy she'd had no idea what would be waiting for her when she woke up. Her mother could be lying unconscious on the floor and, worse, sleeping in her own urine. Strangers could be in the flat and there was likely to be a pool of vomit somewhere. The flat would be cold, and there was no food in the fridge and no hot water, because Amy spent every last penny on drink and never paid a heating bill. India would always have to wake her mum, and that could sometimes take quite a while. And once Amy was awake, there was no telling what mood she would be in. So India was concerned that she would have to wake me in the morning, like she did her mum, so I reassured her that she needn't worry, I would wake her. I kept my word, and each morning, at 7.30 a.m., I knocked on her door, respecting her space.

'Time to get up, India. Here's some warm milk.'

People wonder how long it takes to love the damaged children who come into our home, and the honest answer is that I can love some straight away and have

44

an immediate connection with them that happens with little or no effort, while with others it can take me months to love them and for them to love me. And with some the bond just doesn't come, no matter how hard I try. In those cases, I am pretty sure the child tries just as hard, which is why it is so sad. And like Martine, I was finding it hard to bond with India.

She hid behind an impenetrable wall of steel and it took us years to break through it. I did everything I knew that kids loved to do. We went clothes shopping and I would tentatively hold her hand as we walked through the park, but inevitably she would pull away. We cooked together. Cake-making is sometimes a miracle worker. Believe me, I am a terrible cook and most of the time the children lead me. We often burned the buns and had the smoke alarm ringing in our ears, but we laughed and tried again. I knew that the one thing I could not do was scream and shout, because that was exactly what India expected.

It was important for India to see that if I did raise my voice it was okay, I would still love and care for her, and nothing terrible would happen. Her school uniform would still be ready for her, her breakfast would still be on the table, she would still get a kiss on the cheek when I said goodbye and, more importantly, I would come back to get her, unlike Amy, who was forever forgetting to collect her.

Consequently, India was suffering from attachment disorder, which for her meant that she steered clear of adults, rather than gravitating towards them, when she needed to feel safe. Martine had started the process of helping India to trust adults but had struggled. Hugging a child who is like a brick wall is disconcerting and, as a carer, you start to question what you are doing wrong. To a lesser degree, I was no different, but I had to remind myself that caring is all about giving to them and not wanting or needing anything back, unless of course they want to give love and affection to you.

My initial reaction if India fell over or started crying was to run over, pick her up and cuddle her, but the minute I touched her she would go rigid until I let her go. She was a pretty little girl, too, and sometimes I wanted to hug her for no reason, but the minute an arm went round her shoulder she turned as stiff as a fence post.

After this happened a good few times and there was no change, I had to take a moment then to question my own actions and intentions. Was it that I needed a hug, rather than India? And if I needed a cuddle, maybe I had to recognise that India just didn't. I began to realise that there was an overpowering mother hen in me and that this little girl just did not like it, so I reined myself in.

The girls asked on several occasions: 'Why doesn't India like kisses, Mummy?'

I would answer: 'Because the fairy kiss-mother missed her on her rounds of handing out kisses, but one day she will find India, get her magic wand and sprinkle her with special kisses. From that day on, India will love having a kiss goodnight.'

I would tell India this story, too, and she loved it and asked me to repeat it over and over again, but she never asked me for a cuddle.

I did make some breakthroughs, though, and when I did I received a much-needed confidence boost that I was doing things right.

One of my favourite afternoons was to head to the forest with Martin, the dogs and the children, and romp around in the autumn leaves. I love the smell of winter in the air as it starts to turn cold, the reds and golds of the leaves and the crunch they make under foot. On these family days the kids and dogs would race off ahead, Jack and Jill chasing the children and Martin and I enjoying a rare opportunity to chat together.

One Sunday afternoon, Isabella was in the buggy and we tramped through the forest at a leisurely pace. Suddenly the peace was shattered by a shriek from Francesca, who came running over, breathless and panting.

'Mum! Come quick, India's fallen over. There is so much blood!'

Francesca is the family drama queen, so I knew every minute detail of India's accident before I arrived on the scene. She'd tripped over a tree root and gashed her leg, which to listen to Francesca you would have thought was almost severed.

I didn't know what to make of the scene when I got there, because on the one hand it was lovely to see Ruby cuddling India so tightly; on the other, Ruby was cuddling India so tightly her face was almost obscured, but I could just about see that tears were streaming down her face. What was plain to see was the blood gushing from a deep cut on her knee. India had fallen before but usually she jumped up before I got there and never shed a tear. This time was different. India didn't hesitate; she looked me in the eyes – she rarely made eye contact – and stretched up her arms, wanting me to pick her up.

It was an intimate moment we had both been waiting for and I didn't pause.

'Darling,' I whispered, wiping her tears. 'You are going to be okay. Let's go home, clean your knee, have a cuddle, a hot chocolate and a biscuit.'

India nodded, wrapped her legs around my waist and put her arms around my neck, holding me so tight, as if she never wanted to let go.

I felt euphoric and could not stop smiling for the next couple of hours.

Martin winked at me and said, 'You're getting there, love, you're getting there.'

A couple of weeks later, India picked up the colouring pens for the first time. I held my breath, didn't look and carried on washing up. When she finished, I asked, 'Can I see?'

India nodded. On the paper, she had drawn a picture of a house, garden, dogs and trees and she was standing next to the house, smiling.

'India, that's lovely!' I said, trying to hide the tear running down my cheek.

She nodded, smiled, and ran away before I could cuddle her.

Chapter Five

Amy was convinced there was a reason for India's 'coldness', a reason that made me want to cry. She was certain a fourteen-year-old cousin had touched India. She had said as much to social services, but nothing had been proved, and India had never made a complaint. Amy went on about it for years, though.

As the months passed and I got to know Amy better, I found out there was a good reason for this. What I heard made me so angry I wanted to weep.

Amy had her own troubled past. She was the youngest child from a big family, brought up on a council estate in Manchester. Their alcoholic father was killed in a drunken brawl one night, leaving Amy's mum with seven children under ten to care for. She married again a few months afterwards and moved to London when Amy was a toddler. The family made their home on a rough council estate in South London, but Amy never forgot her dad. She talked about him as though he was a hero, which was a complete fantasy, as he was clearly never a knight in shining armour – he used his family and never provided for them. If he came through the front door, Amy's mum knew that he needed cash or a bed for the night, and if there was anything in the fridge he would have that, too.

Idolising her dad distracted Amy from the sexual abuse she was suffering at the hands of her step-father, Mike.

There was no doubt in Amy's three-year-old mind that the abuse was her fault. She knew she was to blame, because Mike told her that she was time and time again.

'If your poor mummy found out what you made me do she would cry. You must never tell her, because she would be upset and you would have upset her.'

Then he would say, 'You're a dirty little girl. You like this, don't you?'

'I don't, Mike, I don't,' Amy would cry.

Then he would threaten her. 'You do this, you dirty little cow, otherwise I'll kill you. If you let me do this to you then I'll leave your brothers and sisters alone.'

How could she defend herself against that monster?

Mike's threats were venomous, evil. There was not an ounce of compassion in the man. His only thought was for his own satisfaction and manipulating Amy into silence. He was a liar, too. It didn't matter what Amy did; he never left her brothers and sisters alone, except perhaps for one ...

How Amy survived I have no idea, but she endured this abuse for two years before her brother Luke came home one Sunday afternoon and opened the bedroom door to find five-year-old Amy masturbating Mike. Luke told her later that he had fought the urge to run to a get a meat cleaver to cut off Mike's dick, but he thought better of it and had the presence of mind to call the police. After that, the system took over and all the children were placed on the 'at risk' register.

Mike was arrested, charged and sentenced to eighteen months, but when he came out of prison he came straight back to live with Amy's mother, Kathleen, and it wasn't long before the abuse started all over again. It seems incredible but Kathleen knew what was happening and did nothing to stop it, though Amy always defended her.

'She was just frightened, Mia. He was a bully. She couldn't stand up to him.'

I thought how I would have fought like a lioness if any man had tried to touch my children.

But Mike *was* a very violent man. Kathleen was rightly terrified of him and felt powerless against him, so he just carried on as though it was his right, and no one dared stop him.

He liked young children of either sex, and the younger the better. As the youngest, Amy got the worst of it and was raped several times before her sixth birthday.

It was the Seventies. Child sex abuse was rarely discussed or thought about by decent families and its catastrophic impact was just coming to light. It sounds terrible to say this, but it wasn't really taken that seriously, and often children who complained were told they were lying, so you can imagine how childhood for Amy was a never-ending round of torture. The terror she must have felt each time she saw him is unthinkable. She would have had no concept that anything could be different, and nothing ever was – in fact, it only ever got worse.

I never met Mike, but I was told that to look at he was just like any other bloke you might meet in the pub. I thought he would be brutish and dangerous-looking, but apparently he was a bit like an office worker, a wiry man with a moustache and glasses, someone you wouldn't have looked twice at in a crowd.

I could never understand why Amy's mum allowed him back in the house, but he did come back and it was another two years before social services found out what was happening. This time they removed all the children, placing them in children's homes, deciding that Kathleen was incapable of caring for them. That might have been true, but to the kids that equalled punishment, not protection. In their eyes, Mike was more important than they were.

The worst thing was that it could have stopped there if the law had done its job properly, but Mike was arrested, charged and given another pitiful eighteen-month sentence. The family were split up, Amy was separated from Luke, whom she absolutely adored, and was sent into residential care, alone.

Once Mike was released from prison for the second time, he threatened to come and get her and was spotted a number of times outside her children's home and school. When Amy was twelve, and when everyone's guard was down, he caught her, dragged her into his car, took her to a wood and raped her. When he'd finished, he bundled her back in the car telling her, 'You bitch! That's for having me put away.'

There was to be no end to her nightmare, but she discovered that if she drank, it numbed the pain and fear. So from the age of fourteen she began drinking herself senseless, and the care home saved her life on several occasions. Deep down, Amy had no desire to live. Actually, the truth was, she had no idea *how* to live, and saw death as the only solution to her problems.

She did say that the children's home saved her in many ways, but she felt abandoned there because her family only rarely came to see her. Her mother was supposed to visit every three weeks, but sometimes she didn't turn up and at other times Amy didn't want her to come because Mike would be sitting in the car.

Before long, Amy was bunking off school and walking round the streets, drinking strong lager and buying as many cans as she could with the guilt money her mother gave her. By the time she was eighteen and ready to leave care, she was drinking all day every day, and when she found herself in a flat by herself, with no carers to guide her, she had no idea how to deal with life and her drinking got worse. She was effectively abandoned at eighteen, like an injured, frightened animal, almost beyond saving.

Amy's family were all very alike: dark hair, blue eyes and hard, battered faces. They looked like they had experienced a lot of pain, all except for Luke, who had blond hair and brown eyes. He was slim, well dressed, stood tall and had a completely different outlook on life. He never touched alcohol, ever, whereas the others all seemed to be addicted to drink. Luke was the only sibling who didn't fall foul of the law and never had his children taken into care.

In Luke, there was not much family resemblance at all, and it was his son that Amy accused of touching India. I always wondered whether it was jealousy on Amy's part and whether she wanted to find a way to spoil his life so that he had to struggle like the rest of them. They had been so close when she was little, but that attachment had been broken long ago by the system.

A dignified tower of strength, he rose above it all and was a loving and concerned uncle who visited India twice a month, always arriving with a present, usually a book, as he knew she loved them. Luke's was the only face India had looked forward to seeing when she lived with Amy. Luke arriving meant she could escape from Amy's wretched flat to spend an afternoon in the park. Luke arriving meant the washing would be done and the flat tidied a little, and Luke meant dinner and, most importantly, safety. Luke's face held positive memories, of which India had precious few.

'Hello, Uncle Luke. Have you got me a book?' she would say when he came to our house, and Luke would produce a new one from his bag.

The two of them would settle down on the sofa and he would listen intently as India spoke about what she had done at school and what books she was reading. You could see he desperately wanted her to have a better life.

I had a lot of time for Luke and I wondered if he had survived because he had escaped the sex abuse. I never found the courage to ask him, but his demeanour, everything about him, suggested his life had been easier.

When India was eight, however, Luke's youngest son was killed in a terrible accident on the Underground and after that all contact with India ceased. It was years before I saw Luke again. He was

a broken man and I wondered just how much heart-
ache one family could take. When he stopped visit-
ing, India became quite subdued for a while. It was
another kick in the teeth for her and she put another
brick in the wall she was building to protect herself
from the agony of life.

When India had first arrived in care Amy was
allowed contact every three weeks. I had met her
once with Martine when they were out shopping and
just said hello, but didn't notice much about her.
The next time we met, India was in my care and we
were at the social services offices. She didn't make
much eye contact, was quite aggressive and her body
language, with her arms and legs firmly crossed, said
she didn't want to be there at all.

She was interested in India's future, though, and
how living with me was going to affect her. She
asked lots of questions and wanted to know all
about the other children in the house, whether I
had any pets and if I had a garden. She was
concerned that India should have some continuity
and could stay at the same nursery, so she obviously
cared for her in her own way. Her main concern
was that India be protected from any men who
might sexually abuse her, so she asked a lot of questions about the men I knew, and which men would
have contact with India. I left the meeting with no
strong feelings about her either way. I had seen it

all before and Amy was nothing out of the ordinary.

As a mother, Amy was demanding and chaotic, and I often told her she couldn't see India if she turned up stinking of drink.

Children in care love it if their foster carer gets on well with their parents, so when Amy was sober enough to visit, I was happy to see her. India was happy to see her, too, but equally relieved when she went home. When she waved goodbye, she never shed a tear or asked, 'When is Mummy coming back?'

Amy was skinny as a rake – she barely ate – and looked twenty years older than she was. Her blue eyes were generally bloodshot, her face ruddy and her dark brown hair was a mess. There was usually more than one stain on her clothes somewhere and her shoes were always falling apart. She never wore a coat, either, even when the temperatures dropped and it was snowing.

'I never feel the cold, Mia,' she would say.

People like Amy, who have been through so much, have the gift of being able to work people out quickly, and will use that knowledge to manipulate you. Amy was very good at this; it was a skill she had mastered when growing up, as getting her own way allowed her some control over her chaotic life.

She would put on such a good act she could have won an Oscar. She learned the knack when she was a child. When her brothers and sisters needed booze, they would send her knocking on neighbours' doors to ask for food. As the youngest, she had more chance of being believed and of coming home with a few quid. She told me how she would stand at a neighbour's door, bottom lip quivering, a tear creeping down her cheek, and you would have had to be totally heartless to ignore her.

At school she said she learned that if she got angry in the classroom, someone would take her out of the class and give her one-to-one attention. In the care home she would wreak havoc, accusing others of bullying her, and to make it up to her the staff would treat her to a cinema night or take her bowling.

She learned to play the system and wrapped most social workers round her little finger. Attention was as important as booze to Amy; the more police cars, social workers and people she could draw in when she had a little drama, the better she liked it.

She knew why her life had gone so wrong. Childhood is a chance to grow up and learn how to cope in an adult world, but Amy had never had that. Her childhood and teenage years were about survival and finding oblivion. Once she hit eighteen and was expected to leave the care system and look after herself, she realised she had no skills to cope and it went downhill from there. Amy was institutionalised and reliant on other people to care for her; independence was never going to work.

Yes, Amy had neglected India, but once I knew what she had been through as a child, I was full of admiration that she even attempted to go on living. Amy was a consequence of a failed system. Everyone who could have protected her hadn't, and her life would always be a mess because she had no grounding. She was a grown woman, but reaching eighteen doesn't magically wash away the past and provide you with a future.

I always wondered whether her insistence that India had been abused was in fact her way of working through the abuse she herself had suffered as a child.

As easy as India was to care for, Amy was the opposite. I knew my role was as India's carer, but my nature is to care full stop, and I thought if I could help Amy put her life back together, that would help her form a relationship with India. What I did not know then was what a massive job looking after Amy would become. I became her mother, therapist, Samaritan, lifeline and soul mate. I tried to take a step back, but the harder I fought, the harder Amy fought to drag me into her life. She could see I wanted to help her – help she so obviously wanted – and she was not going to give that up easily. To me, she was another lost soul.

I took Amy under my wing, although I was cautious – there was no open-door policy, and we met at cafés or the park, places where Amy felt secure telling me about her life. I didn't judge her; I just listened.

I don't know whether or not this is a fault but I find it impossible to turn my back on someone who is suffering. It is so easy to get dragged into situations without realising, and before you know it, you're in over your head. Being Amy's unofficial therapist was never an intention, but our conversations lifted her spirits, I could see that. At the same time, she was in a dark place and was pulling me down with her.

It was on one of these walks that I first spoke to Amy about India's hair.

'Amy, the nits were so bad you could see them jumping out of her hair.'

She went silent and pale, but as we strolled along the path she explained why she hated India's short hair.

'I had long, beautiful hair when I was little and Luke used to brush it for me. I loved it when Luke did that. But when I was six I cut it all off with the kitchen scissors,' she said. 'I thought the creature would leave me alone if I did.'

I looked at her. She was crying, and before long I was crying, too.

Amy's life was so complicated it was hard to keep up. Drink had become her lifeline and provided an escape from her childhood nightmares, but it only numbed the pain for short periods and at other times would exacerbate it. Sometimes Amy was drunk all day and all night, and went missing for days on end. Then I would usually get a phone call from a police station or hospital, with Amy in the background slurring, 'Get Mia. I'm going to kill myself.'

I would frantically phone her brothers and sisters, panicking, saying that they needed to find her, and at the time I could never understand why they were all so calm when Amy was about to commit suicide.

The first time she threatened to throw herself out of her window, I was crying and saying, 'Wait, I'll come and get you.' I raced round to the estate where she lived, which was a pretty reasonable one: it was full of low-rise flats and some residents had tried really hard with their gardens, while others had flowers growing on their balconies. Amy's balcony was full of junk, though.

It wasn't long before I spotted her sitting on the window ledge of her fourth-floor flat. She was so drunk I could barely understand a word she was slurring. After racing up the stairs, I walked in as calmly as I could. Her lounge was full of police and neighbours looking concerned and anxious, and Amy, the centre of attention, was screaming that she wouldn't talk to anyone but me. She felt secure with me because I didn't panic or scream when I was with her, but I felt like screaming now. I wanted to holler: 'For God's sake, Amy, come back in! Killing yourself won't make it any better.'

I stayed calm, though, and gently asked everyone if they could go into the kitchen and leave us alone. I had to think fast, and before I realised it I was speaking to her as though she was sitting next to me having a cup of tea, not hanging out of the window about to kill herself. I related the true story of David, a distant relative who had suffered with depression for years and threw himself off a sixth-floor balcony.

'But David did not die, Amy,' I said. 'He was para-lysed instead and has no feeling from the waist downwards. That jump put him in a wheelchair and he was reliant on everyone else to look after him. All the things he had taken for granted, like playing football in the park with his children, were distant memories.'

I looked and Amy had calmed down, although tears were streaming down her face.

'Amy, do you want to end up in a wheelchair?' I said. 'You probably won't kill yourself, and I can't look after you because I'm too busy.'

After that, she turned round, took my hand and climbed back inside. We cuddled and smiled at each other. The police looked relieved and sat down on the stained sofas. With my heart in my mouth I managed to say, 'Shall we all have a cuppa?'

As I walked away, I realised that Amy was testing me to see how far I would go for her. I think that's what her suicide attempts were all about – finding out who cared. I cared, but I would never do that again. I wasn't qualified to deal with anything on this scale, and resolved to tell Amy when she was in a better frame of mind.

For all Amy's faults, I knew that I genuinely did love her, even though she was unpredictable and you never knew which Amy you were going to get.

So when she called a few weeks later, I said, 'Let's meet for breakfast at our normal café.'

I turned up at Joe's on the high street to find Amy sitting in the corner.

'You look like crap,' I said, smiling as I realised I sounded exactly like Janet.

'I don't feel well.'

'What do you expect? Your lifestyle means you are going to feel ill and will probably die young.'

'I'm pregnant,' she announced, just as the waitress came to take our order. 'Full English …'

'Don't forget to say please,' I prompted.

'Full English, please.'

'I'll have the same, please,' I said to the waitress. 'Who is the father?' I asked Amy when the waitress had gone.

'I don't know.' But I suspected she did.

The act of sex had no meaning to Amy. It was never something she received with love. She would use sex to get something she wanted or needed, like another drink, but that came at a cost.

I was not impressed and a horrible angry feeling began to well up inside me. For a split second I bit my tongue, then I said, 'Are you mad, Amy? You can't look after the child you already have.'

Our breakfasts arrived and were plonked down on the table.

'What do you know?' she said, looking me in the eye.

'I know that you are selfish and don't want to help yourself. You have become a victim and want to stay like that. People give up on you because you don't want to help yourself, and the devastation you leave behind is exhausting!'

I got up and walked out, paying the bill as I left. I knew I had been harsh, but someone had to say something.

Two weeks later, Amy called to say she'd had a miscarriage. Was I meant to feel sorry or guilty? I suspected Amy was lying and later found out she had terminated the pregnancy. Now I knew exactly how to feel: full of sorrow.

Amy did have a long-term boyfriend called Archie, whom she pushed in and out of her life when she felt like it. Archie was resilient, though, and when Amy let him he was the one person who had been in India's life since she was born.

He had a kind face, wrinkled from spending too much time in the sun, and although he wasn't tall he stood tall. His laugh was infectious and he always had a smile on his face, but the best thing about him was that he was teetotal.

India called him Dad and it was obvious that he loved her very much and that she loved him. Archie was one of the few men she looked comfortable around.

He was ten years older than Amy and looked like the father figure she so desperately needed. You would have thought having found her knight in shining armour she would have melted into his arms, but she gave Archie the run-around, and he seemed to love it.

Archie lived in a council flat on a very rough estate but was respected by all. I could feel his presence was known when I walked round there with him. No one robbed his flat, touched his car or crossed him. His kindness was unconditional, but you just knew not to cross a line.

Why he fell in love with Amy I have no idea, because by now she was the most demanding, problematic woman I had ever known. She was forever getting into arguments, getting picked up by the police, threatening suicide and getting herself sectioned. Nonetheless, Archie stayed loyal to her and to India.

I honestly believe that Amy loved Archie, too, and although he stayed away when India first came into care I often heard Amy speak about him. It was

Archie this and Archie that, and I was curious and intrigued to meet anyone who was willing to take Amy on. Most people gave up pretty quickly.

People who tried to help Amy usually failed: psychiatrists, family members, lovers, me, Archie … Amy had a self-destruct button and sabotaged anything good in her life. She did not want to help herself, but the problem was that Archie and I were hooked on trying to get Amy back on her feet, or at least into a comfortable sitting position. Neither of us had any intention of giving up.

Chapter Six

A new year began and brought hope and fresh starts for a lot of people, but it brought scandal to Amy.

It was a gloomy, grey afternoon and nothing much was happening when there was a knock at the door. I opened it and was surprised to see five angry-looking police officers staring at me. I stood there, not really knowing what to say, but before I could speak an officer said, 'We have a warrant to search your premises.'

I was stunned. My mouth opened but nothing came out, and before I could say anything they pushed past me. All I could think was thank God India and the girls were at school.

A detective took me to one side and told me in a stern voice that they had information that I was keeping Amy Matthews safe.

'I look after India, not Amy,' I said, feeling confused.

They began searching the house, which set off Jack and Jill who began barking their heads off. All I could do was follow them from room to room while they spoke to each other and ignored me, exchanging glances each time they finished and moved onto the next. I felt like a suspect in a police drama and wondered what I had done wrong.

When they had finished searching they asked if I knew where Amy was.

'No,' I said. 'Why?'

They didn't answer. All they would say was that it was very serious and that I should get in touch if she came by.

'I will,' I replied.

Once they'd gone, I ran round the house closing all the cupboards they had left open and shutting the attic door.

I had never experienced anything like it. I had never been on the wrong side of the law or been raided by the police, but the way they were acting made me feel as though I was a criminal.

It was an uncomfortable feeling. I was agitated and couldn't concentrate on anything. Until now, I'd only ever seen the side of the police that was there to help, but the way they had barged into my house with absolute authority was terrifying. There were no smiles, no banter, no one was going to stay for a cup of tea, and although none of them had threatened me, they left me in no doubt that if they found me culpable in some way they would come down on me and my family like a ton of truncheons.

It felt like I was in the middle of a bad dream, real but alien at the same time.

The only thing that kept going through my head was, 'What on earth has happened?' I drove myself mad trying to guess. Surely they would have told me if Amy had attempted suicide again, so it must be something else.

I called Amy's mobile but there was no answer. It mostly just rang and rang and at other times it was unobtainable. I kept calling all night and never got an answer. The next day I decided to call Luke. I knew I had his number somewhere and pulled out every drawer in the house until I found it. He picked up the phone immediately.

'Luke, it's Mia.'

'Oh, hello, Mia,' he said quietly.

'The police have been round looking for Amy.' Luke went silent and then I heard him sobbing.

'They are looking for Amy because our step-father, Mike, has been murdered,' he said.

I was stunned. Mike lived on a notorious estate, full of grimy tower blocks connected by stretches of grass. There were areas for kids to play but none of them did – they were too scared to, as drug dealers and winos hung out there. It was littered with old prams and rubbish and was a depressing place to live, but apparently Mike liked it because his flat overlooked a children's playground, the one place on the estate where mothers could take their toddlers to the swings.

It was a Saturday night and he'd been five miles away at a pub he liked to go to, full of horrible, mean men just like him. What he didn't spot was two men shadowing him all night. He left about midnight, the worse for wear, and staggered home, stinking. All you would have been able to smell if you walked behind him was drink, cigarette smoke and sweat. Those were the three things Amy said she remembered most about him.

He had no idea he was being followed until he got back to the estate and one of the men stopped him and asked for a light. While Mike fumbled in his pockets, anxious to oblige, the other one grabbed him from behind and slit his throat. It was over in seconds and Mike bled to death before the ambulance arrived. The men disappeared and although they were spotted running away, everyone on the estate said they had no idea who they were.

I was so shocked I couldn't say a word. I kept opening and closing my mouth but no words would come out, and as I quietly digested what Luke had just said, the phone went dead.

I knew I had to tell Martin later, and was dreading his reaction. In the end, he said very little. His main concern was that we were all okay, and then he looked me in the eyes and said, 'Mia, this is serious. Amy could have had something to do with Mike's murder. I know we all think that's what we would do if he'd made us suffer like that, and plenty of people wanted him dead, but that's not how it's done. We can't take the law into our own hands, otherwise the world would just start going backwards.'

I knew he was right.

'Evil' was the word most used about Mike and I could not deny that part of me felt happy he was gone, because now hundreds of children would be safe from him, but at the same time all I could think was, 'Could Amy have done it?' God knows she had a motive and so did her brothers, but could she actually have been involved in a cold-blooded murder?

When I said the word in my head it was followed by the sudden realisation that I was involved in a genuine murder investigation. I was on the periphery, certainly, but the only person I had never met in the whole horrific saga was Mike. I knew the other suspects – Amy's brothers – so it was no wonder the police had raided the house. I kept having flashbacks. I prided myself on being law-abiding, and although the police had not been aggressive, they had been brutally efficient, opening cupboards, searching the girls' bedrooms, our bedroom – they had even checked to see whether there was access to the roof. I felt dirty and tainted and began to cry.

One thing I was dreading was Amy turning up and confessing. What the hell would I do then? The minute I had the thought I knew I would persuade her to hand herself in. But what would I do if she refused? I couldn't think about it.

The following days were full of stress and anxiety, as I knew that Amy could turn up at my door at any time. She phoned a few times and each time I noted down her number and passed it to the police. I was living on my nerves for those few days, wondering where Amy was and when she would get in touch. Then I got a phone call from India's social worker.

'Amy and her brothers have been arrested,' she said. 'They are being questioned about the murder of their stepfather.' I could feel the colour draining from my face and thought I might faint.

The story hit the front pages of the papers and more police officers came round asking questions, followed by more social workers asking yet more questions. I was totally confused.

I went over and over every little detail Amy had told me. I knew she hated Mike, but I questioned whether she was capable of murder. I wondered what frame of mind she was in and, more importantly, what the future would be for India.

After the arrest, I was told by the police as well as social services that all contact with Amy was to cease, and India was not allowed to see her either. My job at that time was to protect India from what was going on and I resolved that that was what I was going to do.

It was a difficult conversation but I had to sit India down and tell her. I am a firm believer in telling children the truth, but there are exceptions and this was one. How do you tell a six-year-old that her mother is being investigated for murder?

I waited until Ruby and Francesca had gone to their drama class that evening and I knew I would have some time with India alone. I'd packed a snack and a juice carton in their bags and waved as their friend's mum came to collect them. They were having a sleepover and I had promised India that we would watch a DVD later with Isabella. I said we could have popcorn and lemonade and I knew she was really looking forward to it.

India looked so cute in a pair of pink tracksuit bottoms and with a big heart on her T-shirt and I thought about what I would have to tell her later.

As she settled down in bed that night, I said, 'India, I have something to tell you.' Her eyes grew wide. 'Mummy won't be able to see you for a while.'

Most children break down if someone tells them they can't see their mum, but India didn't even flinch. She accepted my explanation, picked up her book and began to read. The only hint that she was hurting was the way she clutched her Velveteen Rabbit toy, which I had bought her for her fifth birthday, but other than that, she showed no emotion. Amy had let her down so many times, why should she get upset?

All she said was: 'Night-night, Mia, don't let the bed bugs bite.'

* * *

It was a couple of weeks later that I spotted Amy on the corner of my road, leaning against a tree. She looked terrible, like she hadn't slept for days, and her jeans were covered in mud and grass stains, so I guessed she'd been sleeping rough and probably drinking all night. The stench of alcohol hit me long before I reached her.

'Are you okay?' I asked.

She nodded and kept her head down.

'Come on, Amy, let's get you a cuppa.'

I had no time to think I shouldn't be doing this, or I must call the police and social services. I followed my heart, and if ever I was needed it was now. Society had let Amy down so many times and I wasn't going to turn my back on her.

I had no time to think that my foster-care career could be over, because I knew I could be struck off for not calling them immediately. I would call, but first I thought it was right that we sat down and talked. Social services might see it differently.

I comforted myself knowing that I had been diligent about writing up contact reports each time Amy had visited India at my house. I had been honest if I had any concerns. After this drama blew up I had attended every meeting and made sure I gave the police and social services all the information I could, no matter how small. While Amy was on the run I had logged her phone numbers when she'd called me and handed them over to the police, and thanks to that information they had managed to locate her. If social services did have any doubts about me, surely all that would go in my favour?

Once we were home, I made her a hot cup of tea and a bacon sandwich. There was only one question I wanted to ask and I wanted an honest answer.

'Did you do it, Amy?'

'No, but if you'd given me a knife I would have.'

Then she began to tell me in a rush of words and sobs what had happened.

'They arrested us all, Mia. Well, two of my brothers and me. Mike was living in a flat with a new woman who had four young children. We told her what he had done to us and she called us liars. She called me a nutter and told me to go away and leave her family alone.

'How could she let him live there knowing that he was abusing them or was going to? They're just little children, Mia, just little children. We told her that he is a monster, but she wouldn't believe us.'

Thinking of Mike living with three little girls and a boy had haunted Amy day and night, but I knew she did not kill her stepfather. She told me a number of times then that she could have but didn't. She had threatened him and he had called the police, which is why they wanted to question her, but for all her faults she was incapable of murder. It did not mean she was sad he was dead; she wasn't, she was happy, but so were a lot of other people. As one neighbour said: 'We'll be dancing the soles of our shoes off tonight.'

Amy finished her story, turned to me, her grubby face stained with tears, and said, 'He won't harm anyone any more, will he?'

I shook my head and stood there, shaking, with my mouth open. I had no clue what to say. She was right – the man was a monster, and although I don't believe in the death penalty, surely an eighteen-month sentence, which means you are out in a year, is more of a pat on the back than a punishment? It was not justice and not a deterrent, which was why he went on to do it again.

Amy sat there sobbing. I sat in silence next to her, held her hand and prayed.

'You do know that you shouldn't be here, don't you?' I said, aware I was using a tone of voice I would use to speak to a child.

Amy held her head in her hands and I wondered if she had fallen asleep.

'I will run you a hot bath and get you some clean clothes, but I need to call social services and the police.'

'Not yet, Mia, please,' Amy slurred. 'I'm tired.'

She yawned, curled up on my settee and fell asleep. I covered her with a duvet, tucking her in like she was my daughter.

I could not risk being de-registered so I reached for the phone and dialled the police. As Amy had been arrested and questioned already, they thanked me and said they didn't need to speak to her for the time being, asked me to make sure I knew where to contact her and told me to call social services. I let them know they were next on my list and rang off.

Social services urgently wanted to see Amy. I said I would personally bring her to the office tomorrow and would ring them in the morning to confirm. We all knew Amy was unpredictable, though, and that I would be lucky to locate her the next day. Social services seemed happy, however, and said that under no circumstances could Amy see India – she must leave before India came home from school. I reassured them.

When Amy woke up she looked a bit better, and I walked her to the bus stop.

'Don't let me down,' I said.

She nodded, got on the bus and waved goodbye.

I had become protective of her, what with the never-ending phone calls. I hadn't even realised that we had established a bond. It just happened.

Neither Amy nor her brothers were charged with murder, although of the three of them Amy was the most under suspicion. The police were convinced she had paid hit men to kill Mike, but honestly, the most money Amy could ever come up with was enough to buy her next drink.

No murder weapon was ever found and all the Matthews siblings denied they had anything to do with it. They all had a motive, that was certain, but Mike was a prolific sex offender and child abuser, and Amy's family were not the only ones who wanted him dead. No one was ever charged, the case never came to trial and to this day no one knows who killed him.

My one concern was protecting India from all the drama. I'm pleased to say she never found out until she was fifteen, when Amy decided she should know the whole story. They were at my house and when she finished telling her, India wept and broke down.

'Please, Mummy, tell me that's not my dad.'

The release for the Matthews family must have been overwhelming. While Mike was alive, Amy would have gone through a whole raft of emotions over the years: fear, repulsion, hatred, then finally release. The man who sexually abused her and robbed her of her childhood, her mother and her siblings, who had followed her from school and tormented her and raped her in an act of revenge, was finally dead.

Sadly, though, the release had come too late for her and she went downhill rapidly. Constant questioning by the police and talking about the abuse brought it all back. It was never something she could forget, but to have it at the forefront of her thoughts was too much. She had one solution and that was to drink, and drink until she was unconscious. And because she was in such a state, social services decided that all contact with India should cease.

As usual, India showed no emotion. The fact that her mum was no longer a part of her life was neither a relief nor upsetting; it wasn't tragic, it was normal to her. She just went on with her school life, worked hard and her teachers were impressed with her progress. She had a good circle of friends and she concentrated on them.

The police and social services told me not to contact Amy and for once in my life I listened. I had Isabella, Ruby, Francesca, India, Martin and Jack and Jill, and that was enough for anyone. So the next time Amy called I told her I couldn't speak to her.

Amy no doubt saw it as a betrayal and abandonment, but this situation was a whole new ball game. My priorities were my family and India, and that was it. Amy was an adult; India was a child and needed me more. I couldn't put India's needs second yet again. I thought supporting Amy would help India get her mother back, but I was wrong. The opposite had happened. Amy had shouted the loudest, and those who shout the loudest get heard. In all the chaos I had lost sight of the fact that India came first. She would be with us for a long time now that Amy had completely broken down.

Chapter Seven

I wondered if I would ever see Amy again, and then, six months later, social services called me to say they wanted to re-establish Amy's contact with India. They said that Amy had been attending Alcoholics Anonymous meetings, had signed up for parenting classes and had also been to see a therapist. She had tried to kill herself soon after the incident and was sectioned, and once that had happened, the system had taken control. It seemed that in her early forties, Amy was finally sorting her life out.

Amy's social worker, Max, was the one who had turned it all round for her. He was a lovely man who was gentle and kind and had a smile to make you melt.

'Nice to meet you at last, Mia,' he said. 'I have heard so many things about you – all good, I should add.'

He had an inner strength that kept Amy on her toes and meant she could not manipulate him, and to me he was a guardian angel and a miracle worker.

Max was instrumental in the decisions that had to be made in the following years, and it was he who wanted Amy to re-establish contact with India.

India saw her mother for the first time about nine months after the police incident. I prepared her by explaining that Mummy had not been well but that she was better now and really excited about seeing her again. As usual, she showed no emotion. I had never stopped talking about Amy to India – she was not a closed subject – but on this occasion, when I told her, she just kept reading her book as if I wasn't talking.

'Is it okay if Mummy comes on Saturday?' I asked her.

'Yes,' she said, very matter-of-fact, as though I was talking about going to the park. 'We can cook Mummy some dinner.'

Saturday came and Amy arrived with Archie, looking like a naughty child.

'Hello, India.'

'Hello, Mummy.'

Amy looked awkward, and so did India, but they shared a small, fumbled embrace and I knew India was happy. I could tell she loved us all being together.

I put a big buffet on the table, with sandwiches and cakes, chicken and a pasta bake, and things slowly started to fall into place until India felt comfortable enough to tell Amy how much she had missed her. Amy took things slowly, telling her how much she had missed her too. They both sat there with enormous grins.

After lunch, the children went out to play and Amy reached out for my hand, looked into my eyes and said sorry.

'You don't need to say that,' I said. 'I can see you have come a long way and I am extremely proud of you. But you must understand that India is my priority. She needs love, consistency and a mum she knows will always be there for her. She needs unconditional love and I am trying my very best to give her all those things. I am not here to replace you; you are her mother. I will support you and show you what to do, but I ask you one thing: please don't let India grow up thinking you never tried.'

I looked at Amy who had tears streaming down her face. They were real tears – this wasn't Amy turning on an act, she was truly sobbing. I wiped them away. Then she said something heartbreaking.

'I didn't have any of those things, Mia. When I am with you I dream that I could have had a mum like you.'

I felt honoured. When someone calls you Mum it's a sign that they trust you, almost more than anyone else in the world. I cried for the years she had longed for a mother and had nothing but abuse instead. I cried because I know how important families are. But mostly I cried because I could see there was a chance that she could reclaim her own title as mother to India.

I looked at India playing happily in the garden, throwing a ball for the dogs and skipping with Ruby and Francesca. I don't know if Amy took in the significance of the situation, but just then they ran back into the room with the dogs following them, barking.

They played so well together, and Ruby and Francesca were the perfect big sisters. India idolised them. They were her heroes, and she copied their every move. India had learned to be a child, she had learned to be part of a family, and she was learning new skills every day. And I never thought I would say this, but she had a bubbly personality that was beginning to develop.

India had waited years for Amy to behave like a mother. Now, finally, she was, and it was touching to watch the intimacy between them slowly begin to emerge. The first time I realised they were really making progress was when India let Amy brush her hair. India's bob had grown out. Her hair wasn't waist length like before but just passed her shoulders. I was stunned when India let Amy put it in a ponytail and decorate her hair with slides.

Playing with her daughter was difficult for Amy as she had no experience, and I had to smile as I watched her sit awkwardly on the floor with a lap full of Barbies, not quite sure what to do with them. In time, though, she learned how to dress them, and it was sweet to watch the two of them deciding what Barbie should wear.

She helped India tidy her room, putting all the books back on her shelf, and they had the occasional cuddle. They always looked awkward, though, and Amy would catch my eye, as if to say, 'Is this okay?'

She seemed determined to succeed and attended a twelve-week parenting programme with other parents facing similar problems. They discussed anger management and making positive decisions as a parent, what conversations were appropriate to have in front of India and talking to her as a child. That was very hard for Amy to grasp, as she had no boundaries when it came to what was and wasn't appropriate. I worked hard with her, too, explaining about bedtimes, school and personal hygiene. I felt sad that motherhood was so hard for Amy but delighted that she wanted to learn.

Meanwhile, someone had to decide what India's future should be. Amy had come a long way, but with her track record was she capable of caring for India full-time? At meeting after meeting two options were being discussed: should India be adopted or should Amy be given another chance?

India was almost eleven years old and had been in short-term care for seven years now. Max was against

adoption, and at India's age it was going to be difficult to arrange as well.

I thought Amy should be given another opportunity to parent India, to show her a family life,
however imperfect. What was the other option? If
she was adopted it would be a closed adoption with
letterbox contact only with Amy, and however fragile her relationship with her mother was, there were
her aunts and uncles and Archie, whom she adored,
to think about, too. If she was adopted, India would
have to start her whole life again, and who knew
what problems that could cause?

Eventually, the decision was made that India
would move back in with Amy. Before India could
move, though, Amy had to prove that she had a
decent place to live. Amy's track record in this
department was non-existent, but Archie had a
lovely little flat that he turned into a home for them.

When I saw it I was pleasantly surprised. It was
nicely furnished, warm and cosy, and India's room
was decorated with lovely pink wallpaper covered in
flowers. She had shelves to put her books on, a little
bedside light with white frills and a fluffy white rug,
as soft as a cloud, on the floor.

The bed was covered with her teddy collection,
arranged up against the wall. Every single one was
loved and cherished and each one had a memory.
Some were birthday presents or Christmas presents,
and some I had bought when she was unwell to cheer

her up. Some were cuddled more than others and the fur was bare on her most special two. One was a pink bear with a heart sewn onto its chest. Amy had bought it at a funfair at Southend and she was so proud that she had something nice to give India. India called the bear Luke and cuddled him every night. In pole position was the pink Velveteen Rabbit. This bunny had been dragged around by the ears, taken on holiday, sat on beaches, covered in sand and dribbled with Calpol when India refused to take her medicine. The number of times I'd said, 'If Velveteen Rabbit has the first mouthful, will you have one after?'

That rabbit had so many uses; I always suspected its main one was to mop up India's tears when she was feeling confused or low. No wonder it was special.

The move happened gradually, and not until after many, many meetings. Lots of people were at those meetings – all the professionals involved in India's and Amy's lives. There was India's social worker, her teachers, family, Amy's AA support worker, Amy's social worker, our social worker and me. No one was going to make a mistake on this one. Even though Amy had cleaned up her act, there were still risks involved, but everyone reasoned that with Archie's support and her family there as well, Amy would cope. The decision was made: India would go home to her mum, and although I can't deny I was anxious,

I believed from the bottom of my heart that it was what India wanted. If she didn't go home, she would never have her own family, because as much as she had become part of ours, we were only meant to be temporary. I also believed that India would never accept anyone else as her mum, not unless she had been adopted at birth. Whatever Amy's failings were, there was a bond there.

Once the decision was made and India was told, we started to prepare her. Over the last few months she had seen a whole different side to her mother, who was caring, sober and not nearly as needy. Children amaze me how fast they adapt. They live in the moment, so India just accepted without question that her mum had changed. She was excited about going home and began asking, 'When am I going to live back with Mummy? She doesn't drink any more, Mia, so she will be able to look after me properly.'

'Yes, she will,' I said, thinking that it was heartbreaking for any child to make such a statement.

I was hopeful but not 100 per cent sure if Amy could sustain that change, but I liked Archie and I trusted him. He was a solid, reliable man with good morals, so when I was truthful with myself and remembered how unreliable Amy could be I calmed my fears by telling myself that Archie would step in if it all went wrong.

It was time to prepare for the final part of the process which started with India staying with her mum and Archie for four consecutive weekends. On the Friday night she would pack her suitcase – she had a ladybird one now – and her Barbie toiletry case, and get so excited. On Saturday morning Archie would come and get her and he always made a big fuss of her. He would scoop her up into his arms – India being India didn't cuddle him, but she listened intently as he told her what they had planned for the weekend. By now, India had learned to love the seaside, so in warm weather they often headed for the beach.

One thing that made a huge difference to India was the fact that we all got on. There was no bickering, and the relationships were all positive. She absolutely loved that. There was one area, though, that never really changed and that was India and cuddles. She would cuddle me occasionally, because she knew it was something I liked, but I always felt she didn't really mean it. She was tense every time, and that had never changed.

When the month was up, it was time for her to move in with Amy and Archie for good.

We had a big goodbye party and India was allowed to invite anyone who had been significant in her life. There were thirty people on her list and she got very excited at the process.

'Can we have fairy cakes, Mia?'

'Course we can, darling.'

'Can we have orange juice?'

'Of course.'

'Can I have a new dress?'

'I'm sure we can find you something,' I laughed.

We had a barbecue and hired a bouncy castle. There were presents and cards and we took photos to put in her album. Amy and Archie were there and really got involved, and the whole process was as near perfect as you could hope for. My rose-tinted glasses were polished and I was ecstatic that things had worked out as they should. I was realistic, though. I knew Amy still had a journey ahead of her, but it was one I knew she wanted to take. She had come so far and had so much support; I had great faith that she would make it.

When India finally left I felt empty. I had spent seven years thinking about her, caring for her and loving her. It seemed wrong that she was no longer there. It would hit me at different times, like when I called upstairs to say dinner was ready. I would get a feeling of panic, wondering if Amy and Archie knew what she liked for dinner. Then I would tell myself not to be silly – I had already told them what she liked.

Ruby, Francesca and Isabella took it well. There were photos around the house and India phoned two or three times a week and visited once a month – we would have picnics on the green. So although they missed her, they had full lives and a sister whom they adored.

I kept in touch but I also stepped back, as I didn't wish to seem controlling. India started secondary school and things were looking good.

Archie and I knew that Amy had some tough times to come, with no guarantee that she would make it. But she desperately wanted to be successful, and more importantly, India wanted to be with her mum.

'I promise I will be a good mother to India, Mia,' Amy said, and I sincerely believed she would try.

She wanted so much to be a good mum, but her expectations of what a mother should be were extremely low. I had tried to fill in the gaps, as had social services, but we could not be sure it would be enough.

Anyone who lives with an alcoholic lives with hope and clings desperately to that word, because if you don't, all is lost. There was no pretending that Amy wasn't an alcoholic – she was, and alcohol had been a powerful ally to her – but we all hoped that was in the past and that she now had something more powerful to live for.

It might sound tough on India that we could not guarantee the outcome for her, but I knew that children in care who grew up having no contact with their parents spent their whole lives fantasising about their real family. I'd met adults in their fifties who had been adopted by wonderful families and had had happy childhoods, but they always felt that a part of them was missing because they had no idea who their real mother or father was. Family is so deeply ingrained in us that, however hard we try, it's almost possible to eradicate, and like a magnet it keeps pulling you in, for better or worse.

I also knew from my experience of looking after kids in care that if they had no contact with their parents, they put them on a pedestal; they become a fairy princess or a brave knight. Imagine if you grew up thinking your mother was this wonderful human being, only to meet her one day and find out she was an alcoholic like Amy. The shock would be far worse than living with the reality.

I have never worked out why the cards we are dealt are so unfair, but they are. It is a hard fact that some people seem to live a charmed life while others face trauma and tragedies we could not imagine in our darkest nightmares. During my years as a carer, I had come to accept that fact and knew that would never change.

After seven years away from her mother, India was excited to be home – for now. The memories of her early years had faded, and when I waved good-bye I left her with a smile on her face. India was happy that her mum was sober, happy that she had a lovely stepdad and happy with her new home. She couldn't ask for much more.

Whatever the future held for India, she knew that she and her mother had a good relationship with her aunts, uncles and cousins, and no one doubted how much Archie cared about her. We all loved her, and that fact would never change. No one would ever be able to take that love away, and India knew that.

Moving Memoirs

Stories of hope, courage and the power of love…

If you loved this book, then you will love our
Moving Memoirs eNewsletter

Sign up to…

- Be the first to hear about new books

- Get sneak previews from your favourite authors

- Read exclusive interviews

- Be entered into our monthly prize draw to win one
  of our latest releases before it's even hit the shops!

Sign up at

www.moving-memoirs.com

Harper True.
Time to be inspired

Write for us

Do you have a true life story of your own?

Whether you think it will inspire us, move us, make us laugh or make us cry, we want to hear from you.

To find out more, visit

www.harpertrue.com or send your ideas to harpertrue@harpercollins.co.uk and soon you could be a published author.